Speaking Out

Photographs © Patricia Duffin
Greg Wilkinson
Manchester Evening News

Drawings © Kathleen Newsham

John Glynn

Published by The Gatehouse Project

c/o ICI Blackley Works

Crumpsall Gatehouse

Waterloo Street

Manchester 9

Printed by Speedaprint, Hulme Hall Road, Manchester 15

ISBN 0 906253 06 3

The Gatehouse Project thanks:

Manchester Cultural Services

North West Arts

for paying printing costs for this book.

ICI Blackley Works for the loan of

offices in which to work.

Contents

Introduction

This book is a collection

of thoughts and ideas

written or taped by adults

who are learning

to read and write.

A lot of discussion

and argument

went into choosing

these pieces.

You may agree or disagree

with what you read,

but whatever you feel

we hope that these ideas

will spark off discussion

and further writing.

THE PRICE OF WAR
Arzu Miah

There would not be any shortage of food anywhere in
the world, if the big rich powerful countries did not
make any war weapons for using to kill people.

The rich countries like America, Russia, Great Britain, Germany and Japan spend millions and millions of pounds every day on making war weapons and they sell these weapons to the poor countries. If there is war between two poor countries then these big countries get involved in making a peace settlement, but they really do not look forward to making peace. They look forward to keeping the war on, so they can sell their weapons to those poor countries.

Peace-makers

For instance, the war between Egypt and Israel has been going on for a long, long time and the Americans are involved every year in making peace settlements. But after a few talks, they settle for selling jet-fighters, American missiles etc., to both countries. It's mainly to keep the war on, so they can continue selling their weapons.

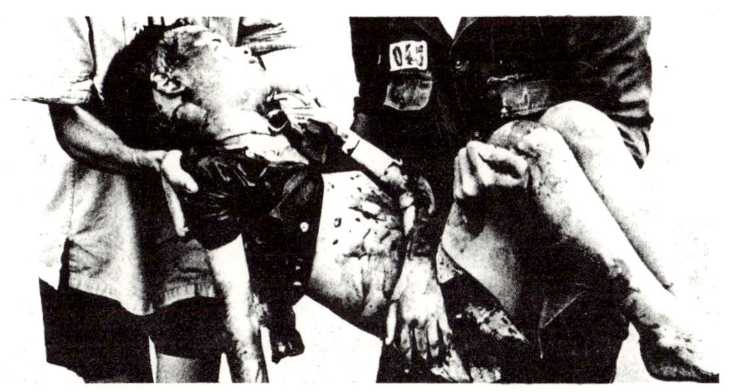

Stop, think

I think the big countries never think about the other people, suffering so many diseases, and shortage of food. If these countries did not have these bad ideas, so many people of the world would not suffer shortage of food, diseases etc.

If these big countries wanted to protect people from suffering for food and by disease, they could easily do that, by spending their money to develop the undeveloped countries, by helping uneducated people to get educated and so on. But I don't think they would ever do that. If they would do that everybody would be happy in this world, nobody would suffer for anything.

ROOM TO GROW

Ronald Pye

Man has built his-self a world in danger.

You get a load of potatoes,

you dig a hole and put them all in it together.

Some grow good, some grow crooked,

some grow down and some not at all.

But if you plant them spread out

they grow good.

People's the same.

Garden City

What I would like to see done

is to change the landscape.

In a city like Manchester,

Crumpsall Hospital and I C I are very big.

If all the buildings was built in small sections

not too far away from each other and not too near,

just in walking distance,

that way there would be less accidents,

such as fires and explosions

because the smaller the things, the less damage,

and less accidents on the road.

Say they split I C I up

so people don't have to travel so far,

and the hospital too.

Anyone takes ill, a hospital will be nearby.

There would be less pollution

and you would not need as much water for the factories.

So all the rivers would become clean again.

Peace and safety

Also there would be less anxiety.

I think most people would like to live

in peace and safety.

But we live in a world of tension and destruction.

It is the way man has built and organised the system.

MAKE IT A STIFF ONE Joseph Hornby

What is an alcoholic? Well to most people he is that dirty scruffy looking character you find sitting on any bench or lying around on some croft,* with a bottle in his hand. People are right to think that of course, but there are some alcoholics that haven't reached that stage yet. Most people find it hard to believe that the well-dressed man or woman in their office could be an alcoholic too.

Danger signs

Society should have a lot more information about this disease in order to recognise the danger signs. There are thousands of people about today who drink far too much but do not consider themselves to be alcoholics; they do not realise they need help to fight their drinking problem.

Always a reason

The man that drinks faster and a lot more than his

            *croft: wasteland

friends, believes he has got it under control; thinking that because he does not drink spirits he is not a heavy drinker. He is only fooling himself since he is still getting alcohol whether it be in beer or spirits. Then there is the man who goes dinner time drinking thinking it will liven him up after the night before or maybe he has two drinks first thing in the morning, always refusing to admit that without that drink he would find it hard to get himself to work at all, but to an alcoholic that type of thinking, kidding oneself, is just to please one's conscience. There are always more reasons which can be found to take a drink.

Under control

In the every-day conversation I have with people at work, the drinking question finally comes around. The reactions of people when you tell them you are an alcoholic, is at first, disbelief, then when they have recovered from the initial shock, some confess to their own drinking troubles, or that of a relation or friend. People show a lot of interest and ask questions about alcoholism until you start to tell them the habits and some of the symptoms of an alcoholic; then they shy away as they start to recognise themselves in what you are saying, and end the conversation by saying ''I drink a lot but I have it under control'' ''I can stop when I want to'' and wonder if they have stopped drinking and for how long. I would give a heavy drinker about three days, after that time he will find a very good reason to have a drink. The excuses he gives himself will be good, but the fact remains that he will be stood at the bar with his drink whatever the reasons! They find reasons, and if they can't find one they will make one,

like deliberately starting a row with someone at home
so that they can storm out of the house feeling really
hurt, then they can go and drown their sorrows in beer;
but they never admit to these sly tricks, it is always the
other people who are to blame, never them. They will
find fault with people at work for nothing, but all that is
wrong is they want a **drink** and cannot get one. They
would be a different person if they could have one, for
the moment, a kind of Jekyll and Hyde person.

The night before

I hear men talking of what a night on the beer they have
had, admitting they cannot remember parts of the night
before, afraid to go back to the pub, not knowing what
they might have said or done wrong.

Blackout

Now in a alcoholic treatment unit, this is called having
Mental Blackouts, and it is a danger sign. There is
nothing funny about it, it isn't a big joke as we try to
laugh it off, we should be very worried. There are

people who just have the odd one or two during the
week, then every five or six weeks they have one big
drinking session that lasts about three or four days.
Now this is called Bout Drinking. The trouble is that the
waiting time gets shorter and shorter and the drinking
time gets longer and longer, until they are drinking
heavy every day.

Help

I think the Department of Health and Social Security
could do far more work than they do for some of the
alcoholics. There is too much of looking on the alcoholic
as a hopeless case and just leaving them in the hope
that maybe some charity may help them along. There
are doctors that do not know enough about this disease.
I have heard of doctors telling their patients to keep off
the bitter beer and just drink mild beer, or of telling
their patients to cut their drinking down which is
impossible for a heavy drinker. If the doctor knew about
alcoholism he could then tell the patient all about it and

where he can get help, because the heavy drinker needs help, he cannot do it alone, he needs treatment when he decides to stop drinking.

First step

I hope that these few words may help someone if they just remember, that once you find you cannot stop drinking, ADMIT IT. If you can do that you are half way home to being a recovered alcoholic.

BUNDLE OF TROUBLE Alan

One of the reasons for children getting into trouble is that parents haven't got enough time to see to their children.

Second point is that life is going too fast for children. Third reason is that the education haven't got much money to spend on playgrounds for children. Most of the ground that is classed as slum clearance is only for building houses and other things on.

The fourth reason is that there is no cinemas for the children to go and watch films in. Years ago children went to the cinemas. They spent most of their time, well, spare-time, in the cinemas watching good films.

These days the cinemas have been changed over to bingo halls.

The children have to make their own amusements. The amusements that they know best is breaking windows, pinching lead, and other things like that.

Another reason for them getting into trouble is that, in my days there was no such a thing as slum clearance. These days, slum clearance has become a place for children to play on. So it brings out the worst in children, and when you get five or six or seven children together, it would surprise you the damage that they can do. One child by itself cannot get into much trouble, but put six together . . .

POLICE

Ron

Many people say the police are doing a good job, and you might reply, 'O yes, it's a good thing Robert Peel organized a police force to keep check on some of the terrible crimes people commit.'

That is true, but he would have done a better job if he had invented some sort of force to keep a look out for some of the terrible crimes the police commit.

Some people talk about the police as though each one was a little tin god. What I would like to see is people, particularly authorities, treating the police as just what they are, human-beings.

16

TOGETHER FOREVER

Mohammed Younis

My name is Mohammed Younis.

I have a brother who lives with me.

We have our mother and one brother in Pakistan.

We both support them.

We will support our mother until she is dead.

If you have got parents you should look after them,

that's your duty,

to look after your parents.

If we look after our parents

our children will look after us.

If we can afford it

we help the relatives as well.

If you help somebody

God will help you.

IT WAS A MAN'S WORLD   Helena Glynn

In the beginning

I think that men are the root of all the trouble that's in the world but this is something they can't help. Right down the centuries ever since the first man, Adam, ate of the forbidden fruit there has been a curse on men. They were looked upon as the cleverest and the brainiest of the animal species. Men were put on a pedestal by their own sex. There is no way of finding out that God made man stronger than women. It was always taken for granted that men were cleverer than women. If you look down the centuries you find that women are mentally and physically fitter than men but they never got the publicity that men got.

Tied to the home

Any woman who wanted to work in a profession was barred from doing so by men. Some men said that men had more brains than women. They thought the only

jobs women could do were cooking, washing and cleaning, and that their brains were only limited to domestic work. They were unpaid servants and they couldn't become doctors or dentists.

Vote or else

There was a very clever woman who was called Emily Pankhurst and her daughters, Sylvia and Christabel — a group of women from all walks of life, who had the courage to stand up for the rights of women. They were called the Suffragettes. This movement has done a lot for women by fighting for the Vote. My opinion is that all women who are of age to vote and do not should be deprived of all rights.

Cigarettes have been banned from television advertisements why not alcohol? People who smoke only do harm to themselves. Well the people who drink do more harm not only to themselves but to other people as well. You get people coming out of pubs walking all over the roads, a right menace to car drivers and all the other road users.

Then you get the man who goes out drinking night after night leaving his wife and family who must go short of money. There is the other man who comes home dead drunk and knocks his wife about so she is forced to go to the battered wives association. If there are children some times the N.S.P.C.C. has to be called in because the children get knocked about.

It's not only men who go in to pubs you get mothers as well because you still can see children playing outside of pubs because the parents are in the pub. If they must still advertise alcohol on television why don't they show

all the harm that is caused by drink? There must be
more things that happen because of drink, I have just
pointed out a few.

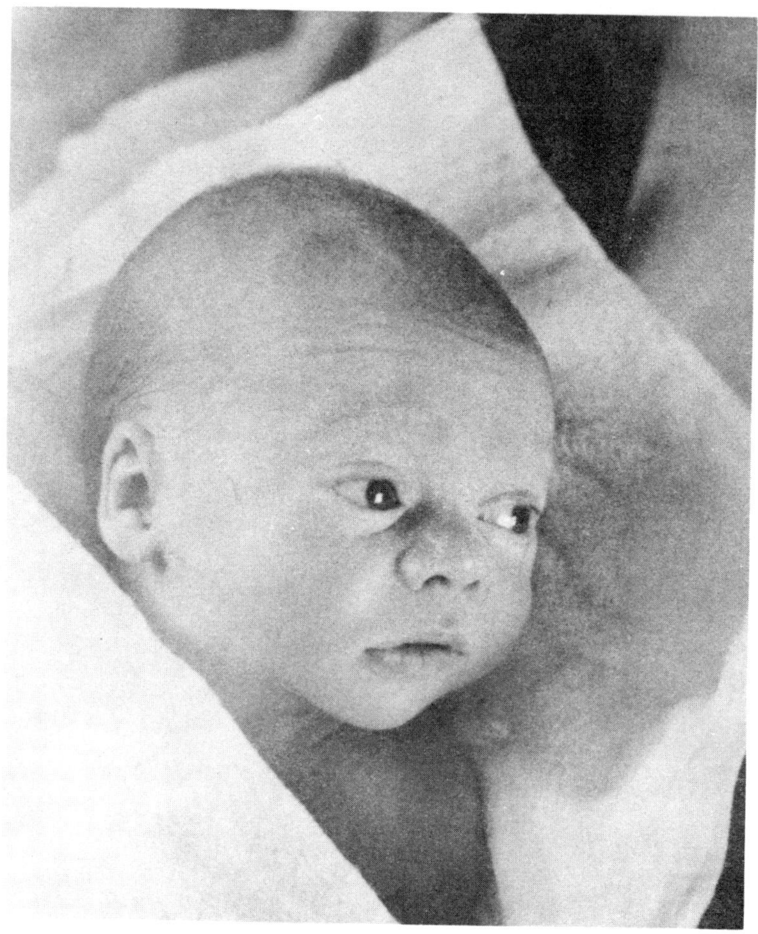

Life is the most wonderful thing in the world. To be

alive, to live day to day and to breathe in the fresh air

into your lungs and to wake up in the morning and see

the sunshine and to hear the birds whistling. That's what life's about, to be able to enjoy yourself. People just don't understand. They waste time. Every day that comes along, time is cut short and you're getting older every year. Every day that you spend is precious. But kids nowadays don't know they're born. They've got it made. They don't care about life or themselves.

Death

But I think that the worst thing can ever happen to you is death. People try not to think about it. It's a horrible thing to happen to anyone, but it does happen. No-one in this world can bring you back. It doesn't matter how much money you've got, that won't save you from dying. That is why you've got to look after your body, and it will look after you. Keep yourself fit. If you smoke, you're asking for trouble. You won't last very long. Smoking can kill. I know that everyone has to die sometime in life, but why do people say to you, ''Don't think about it, you've got a long time yet?'' But how do you stop worrying about it? It's not something you push aside. You hear about young kids dying in fires somewhere, and sometimes you hear of babies dying too. People are dying everyday. But when someone in your family dies or someone you know very well, then it is really hard for you to accept it. You say, ''Why does it happen to them?'' ''If there is a God, why does he let people die?''

Don't kid yourselves

Me myself I don't believe in God. You spend your life going to church, and what for? You hear the priest talk about good and bad, of going to heaven if you're good, but that's a lot of rubbish, There is no such thing as a heaven. They fill people's minds with loads of rubbish. Don't kid yourselves. When you die, you're gone for good, because no-one has ever came back from the dead to tell us what it's like. No-one in this world will ever know until it happens. That's why you've got to love them close to you and do the best you can for them and say what you want to say to them, because when you have done all that, you can be very happy inside,

and what more can you do than that? Some people don't think to do them things till it's too late, because when someone near to them dies they feel bad and they have it on their minds forever.

Forgotten forever

I think to bury you is more decent and proper than to be burnt into ashes. Whatever, it's not nice. They just put you in a box and bury you under the ground. Then the grave-yard becomes your last place in this world. It's cold and horrible and you're alone. You are in peace forever. Then you are forgotten forever. People forget you so easy. Then the grave becomes your home. It is so lonely and empty inside.

Sorrow

But what about children? How do you start to explain to them when their mother or father dies? What reasons do you give? That's what it's all about. Death, sorrow and sadness.

We all need a chance

The people in this life are all in one big rush. They don't know what life is. I am a different person than anyone else. Everyone should have the right to enjoy life, because you only live once. But some people don't get the chance, to do the things they want to do, and that's not right. If people get the chance to do the things they want to do and they are happy with what they have done and that is all they want to do in life, what more can anyone ask for?

The Gatehouse Project is publishing a series of large print books
written by people who have reading and writing difficulties.

Books already published are:
A GOOD LIFE by ALAN 25p
Alan talks about his jobs and how for once reading problems can
be a positive asset in 'How to Get Rich'. A simple text, broken
into short lines, in very large print.   12 pages.

NEVER IN A LOVING WAY: Josie Byrnes 35p
In this moving story of her childhood and the way it affected her
adult life, Josie brings to life the feelings of a child struggling to
cope with hardship and lack of love.   33 pages.

A WOMAN ON HER OWN: Margaret Fulcher 30p
This is a collection of five pieces in which Margaret describes her
life as a woman bringing up a child on her own. A simple text,
broken into short lines, in very large print.   20 pages.

THE DAYS I LIVED IN QUEEN STREET, BURY: Eric Newsham
30p
It was just one row of old houses, but it was always humming with
excitement. There will never be another street like this one. They
have all gone now. This is broken into short lines.   20 pages.

TOMMY COME HOME: Thomas Murray 30p
A young man tells of his adventures from the age of 7 when he ran
away from his home near Dublin. He goes on to describe his
feelings as an adult learning to read.   20 pages.

PAUL THINKS: Paul Harrop 30p
A collection of short witty comments on subjects ranging from
spelling to outer space. This is a very simple text, with only a few
lines on each page and lots of line drawings.   12 pages.

MY OPEN WINDOW: Kevin Mottershead
A book of three poems by a literacy student who has discovered a
great feeling for poetry since joining a literacy group.   25p

Please send orders and enquiries to:

Gatehouse Project
c/o ICI Blackley Works
Crumpsall Gatehouse
Waterloo Street
Blackley
Manchester
M9 3DA

Tel: 061-740 1460
Ext: 2077